WHY
BOYS & GIRLS
ARE
DIFFERENT

For ages
3 to 5
and parents

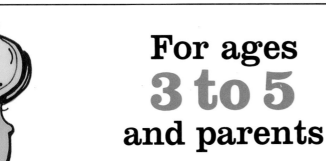

Carol Greene

Book 1 of the Learning about Sex Series

The titles in the series:

Book 1: Why Boys and Girls Are Different
Book 2: Where Do Babies Come From?
Book 3: How You Are Changing
Book 4: Sex and the New You
Book 5: Love, Sex, and God
Book 6: How to Talk Confidently with Your Child about Sex ...
and Appreciate Your Own Sexuality Too

Developed under the auspices of the Family Life Department
Board for Parish Services
The Lutheran Church—Missouri Synod

Illustrations by Maritz Communications Company. Cover design by Concordia
Publishing House.

Copyright © 1982, 1988, 1995
Concordia Publishing House
3558 South Jefferson Avenue
Saint Louis, Missouri 63118-3968

Manufactured in Mexico.

1 2 3 4 5 6 7 8 9 10   04 03 02 01 00 99 98 97 96 95

Editor's Foreword

This book is one of a series of six published under the auspices of the Board for Parish Services of The Lutheran Church—Missouri Synod through its family life department.

Originally published in 1982, the series was updated in 1988, and again in 1995. This 1995 update includes topics of concern that have emerged since 1988.

Books in the series are *Why Boys and Girls Are Different* (Ages 3–5); *Where Do Babies Come From?* (Ages 6–8); *How You Are Changing* (Ages 8–11); *Sex and the New You* (Ages 11–14); *Love, Sex, and God* (Ages 14+); and *How to Talk Confidently with Your Child about Sex ... and Appreciate Your Own Sexuality Too.*

The last book in the series is designed for adults, to help them deal with their own sexuality, as well as provide practical assistance for married and single parents in their role as sex educators in the home.

Why Boys and Girls Are Different is the first book in the series. It is written especially for children at preschool age—and, of course, for the parents, teachers, and other concerned grownups who will read the book to the child. (See the "Note to Grownups" at the end of this book for suggestions on using the book and ways to communicate Christian values in sex education in the home.)

Like its predecessor, the new *Learning about Sex* series provides information about the social-psychological and physiological aspects of human sexuality. But more: it does so from a distinctively Christian point of view, in the context of our relationship to the God who created us and redeemed us in Jesus Christ.

The series presents sex as another good gift from God which is to be used responsibly.

Each book in the series is graded—in vocabulary and in the amount of information it provides. It answers the questions that persons at each age level typically ask.

Because children vary widely in their growth rates and interest levels, parents and other concerned adults will want to preview each book in the series, directing the child to the next graded book when he or she is ready for it.

In addition to reading each book, you can use them as starting points for casual conversation and when answering other questions a child might have.

This book can also be used as a mini-unit or as part of another course of study in a Christian school setting. (Correlated video and study resources are available for both curricular and home use.) Whenever the book is used in a class setting, it is important to let the parents know beforehand, since they have the prime responsibility for the sex education of their children.

While parents will appreciate the help of the school, they will want to know what is being taught. As the Christian home and the Christian school work together, Christian values in sex education can be more effectively strengthened.

Frederick J. Hofmeister, M.D., FACOG, Wauwatosa, Wisconsin, served as medical adviser for the series.

Rev. Ronald W. Brusius, secretary of family life education, Board for Parish Services, served as chief subject matter consultant.

In addition to the staffs of the Board for Parish Services and Concordia Publishing House, the following special consultants helped conceptualize the series: Darlene Armbruster, board member, National Lutheran Parent-Teacher League; Betty Brusius, executive director, National Lutheran Parent-Teacher League; Margaret Gaulke, elementary school guidance counselor; Priscilla Henkelman, early childhood specialist; Rev. Lee Hovel, youth specialist; Robert G. Miles, Lutheran Child and Family Service of Michigan; Margaret Noettl, family life specialist; and Bonnie Schlechte, lecturer on teen sexuality.

Rev. Earl H. Gaulke, Ph.D.

I am he.
God made me.

I am she.
God made me.

God made each one specially.
God made YOU too.
Didn't He do a good job?

I am not like you.

I like to hop.

I like yellow.

I like chocolate
ice cream cones.

I am not like you.
I am ME.
But I like you.

And I am not like you.

I like to jump.

I like red.

I like vanilla
ice cream cones.

I am not like you.
I am ME.
But I like you.

You are not like us.
You are YOU.
God made YOU that way.
But we like YOU.

God gave us eyes
to see with

and ears to hear with

and noses to smell with

and mouths
to taste and talk with.

8

He gave us hands and feet
and fingers and toes
and elbows and knees
and minds to think with.

God made each one of us
specially . . .

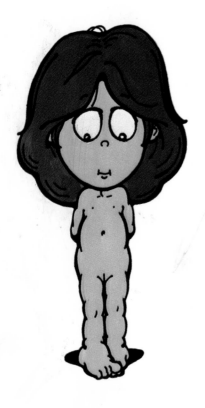

God gave girls
a vagina.
It is on the inside.
That is the best
place for it.

God gave us wonderful bodies.
He gave you one too.

God gave boys
a penis.
It is on the outside.
That is the best
place for it.

God gave us wonderful bodies.
He gave you one too.

You know, God made
a lot of shes,
and shes can do
a lot of things.

My mother
is a she.

So is my grandma
and my cousin

and that nurse

and that banker

TELLER

and that painter

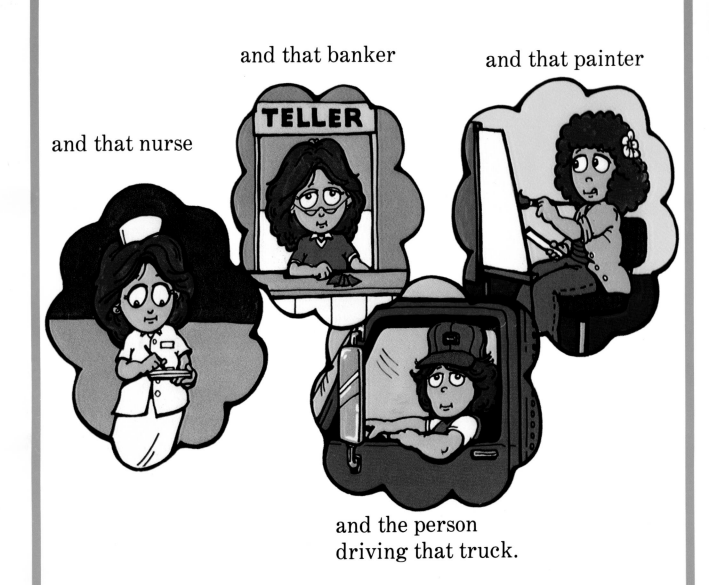

and the person
driving that truck.

I'm glad
I'm a she.

God made a lot
of hes too,
and hes can do
a lot of things.

My father
is a he.

So is my
grandpa

and my uncle

and that lion tamer

and that cook

and that teacher

and the person
flying that plane.

I'm glad
I'm a he.

How did God make us?
I don't know. Let's ask.

God made you
in a special way.
You see . . .

Sometimes a grownup he
and a grownup she
love each other very much.
So, with God's blessing, they get married.
Then they decide
that they want
a little baby
to share their love.

God answers their prayer and then
the baby grows inside its mother
for nine months.
It is safe and warm.
Sometimes it wiggles and kicks.
When it gets bigger,
you can feel it from the outside.

I think that's great!

Me too.

After nine months
the baby is born.
It comes out through the mother's vagina.
The mother and father
are very glad to see it.

That is how God made YOU.
That is how He makes all people.

God does another great thing.
He puts people into families.
That's so they can
take care of each other
and love each other.

Some families are small.

Some families are big.

There are many different kinds of families.

What kind of family
did God put YOU into?

Families do things together.

I like to hug my mother.
She's a good hugger.

I like to play ball
with my brother . .

I like to listen
to my grandma
tell stories.

I'm glad God put me
into a family.

I like to feed my sister.

I like to go fishing with my grandpa.

I like to kiss my father. He feels scratchy, but I like it.

I'm glad God put me into a family.

What do YOU like to do with YOUR family?

God puts us into
a church family too.
People in church
families take care
of each other
and love each other.

Some church families are small.

Some church families are big.

There are many different kinds of church families.

What kind of church family did God put YOU into?

Church families do things together.

I like to make things in Sunday school.

I like to learn about Jesus.

I like to sing songs.

I'm glad God put me into a church family.

I like to see
my friends
at church.

I like
to look
at the
windows.

I like to pray
to Jesus.

I'm glad God
put me into a
church family.

What do YOU like to do
with YOUR church family?

I am he.
God loves me.

I am she.
God loves me.

God loves each one specially.
That is why He is so good to us.
God loves YOU too.
Aren't you glad He does?

A Note to Grownups

We're all aware of the stereotypical adult responses to a toddler's first question about sex. There's embarrassment: "Er—uh—go ask your mother." There's evasion: "Mommy thinks she hears the telephone." And there's the flight of fancy: "Once there was a big white bird ..."

Of course you aren't a stereotype. But you may be one of the many adults who prefer to approach their children's questions with the aid of other resources. This book is designed to provide that aid and to do so in a Christian context.

But no one book can anticipate the needs of all preschoolers. Ultimately, adults must rely on their own sensitivity and common sense. A few pointers, however, may help.

First and foremost, remember that sexuality is far more than the reproductive organs with which each of us is born. It is a tremendous gift from God and colors almost everything we are and do. The sense of joy and wonder you feel in your own sexuality and that of your child is one of the most important things you can teach him or her. And you do it all the time.

"Oh, Daddy," said three-year-old Jessica, twirling before the mirror in her new Easter finery. "I'm so glad I'm a girl!" Joy and wonder were in her eyes, and behind her stood a father ready to rejoice with her.

Ideally, children would grow up in a home with two parents who openly show their love and respect for one another and for their children, where each person in the family is valued for who she or he is. But this isn't an ideal world, and many single parents must cope without the aid of a spouse. If that is your situation, try to spend time with a special friend or relative of the opposite sex and let your child be part of the interaction. Or spend time with a couple in your extended family or church. Models are important for young children.

Now, back to that first question. Even if you are a bit nervous, let your child know that you're glad he or she came to you with it. Curiosity is good; it helps us learn. And bear in mind that a child doesn't carry all the societal baggage attached to sex that adults do. Today Sam wants to know more about his penis. Tomorrow he may show equal curiosity about his teeth.

Listen carefully to the question and be sure you understand it. (Remember the old joke? Bobby asks, "Mom, where did I come from?" Mom gives a carefully preplanned lecture on reproduction. Bobby looks bored. Turns out his best friend came from Memphis, and Bobby just wants to know where he came from.)

Once you understand the question, try to answer it in a precise, matter-of-fact way. If Jenny wants to know why Mrs. Blackwell's tummy is so fat, explain that Mrs. Blackwell is going to have a baby. "But it isn't in her tummy. It's in a special place called the uterus, which God made for babies before they are born."

If Jenny follows this with another question, answer it with equal honesty and continue to do so until her curiosity is satisfied. In general, it's best to answer no more than the child asks. But don't berate yourself later if you think you've said too much. Most small children will absorb only as much information as they can handle.

Don't be surprised, by the way, if Jenny repeats the same series of questions tomorrow or three weeks from now. For a number of psychological reasons, small children thrive on repetition. Be sure, though, that you're consistent in the answers you give.

Also be sure to use correct terminology with Jenny during such discussions. This will let her know that you're taking her quite seriously. It may also prevent embarrassment later.

An area of confusion for some children involves their genitals and their organs of elimination. "They're all in the same place," reasons Sam. "And Mommy says to wash my hands after I go to the bathroom. So they must all be dirty."

If your child thinks like Sam, explain that we wash our hands after going to the bathroom to get rid of any germs that are in a bowel movement. But that doesn't mean that any part of our body is dirty in a bad way. All the parts—penis, anus, ears, and toes—do just the job that God made them to do.

Unfortunately, you should also warn your child about the possibilities of abuse. You might want to work the warning into a discussion of appropriate behavior.

"Your body belongs to you—including those private parts that your swimming suit covers. You don't show those parts or touch them in public. And other people should not touch your private parts either. No one has a right to do that unless it's a nurse or a doctor helping you to be well or someone who cares for you helping you to be clean. If anyone does touch your private parts, be sure to tell me. I promise that nothing bad will happen to you."

Our world is bombarded with sexual references and exploitation. Not even a preschooler can escape that completely. But your child's trust still remains in you. You are the real authority to him or her in almost every matter, including sexuality. Your joy and wonder, respect and love will awaken similar responses in your child. Together you can marvel that "male and female He created them. ... And God saw everything that He had made, and behold, it was very good" (Genesis 1:27, 31).